MW01611344

"Shelby Abbott and *What's the P[...]* research and hi[...] many myths of cohabitation as the 'rehearsal marriage' and then points us to the benefits of a better way, designed for us by a God of wisdom and love. Here is a book that is a quick read but has the power to change a life forever."

PAUL TRIPP, author and international conference speaker

"Shelby Abbott's *What's the Point* is a helpful first-step in showing the problematic fruits of cohabitation. As he demonstrates, the data shows that cohabitation is counterintuitive to stronger relationships. Perhaps this is a sign that cohabitation goes against the grain of the universe."

ANDREW T. WALKER, Ph.D., Associate Professor of Christian Ethics, The Southern Baptist Theological Seminary

"Choices have consequences. Yet so many couples in our day are choosing to move in together prior to marriage without even pausing to consider how that decision might affect their relationship. I'm grateful for this clear-eyed look at some of the pitfalls of living together before tying the knot."

BOB LEPINE, co-host, *FamilyLife Today*; author, *The Christian Husband* and *Love Like You Mean It*

"One of the things that I love about Shelby's book is that his motivation for couples to choose sexual purity before marriage is not based on emotions or preconceived notions. It is based on God's Word and data that backs up the why's behind God's prescriptions."

DAVE WILSON, co-host, *FamilyLife Today*; co-author, *Vertical Marriage*

"As commitment has fallen on hard times, it's no surprise that marriage has as well. Moving in with one's boyfriend or girlfriend prior to—or instead of—getting married used to be culturally taboo. Then it became accepted. Now it is assumed. Only two weirdos would rush into a lifelong arrangement without test-driving it first, right? Wrong. Writing in his characteristic engaging style, my friend Shelby Abbott illumines surprising data that paints a counterintuitive picture: for the best shot at long-term financial stability, sexual satisfaction, and overall relational happiness—not to mention glorifying the God who made you—exchange vows before you share an address."

MATT SMETHURST, managing editor, The Gospel Coalition; author, *Before You Open Your Bible: Nine Heart Postures for Approaching God's Word* and *Deacons: How They Serve and Strengthen the Church*

ASKING THE **RIGHT QUESTIONS**
ABOUT LIVING TOGETHER & MARRIAGE

WHAT'S THE POINT?

SHELBY ABBOTT

FOREWORD BY BRYAN CARTER

FamilyLife Publishing®
Little Rock, Arkansas

What's the Point?
FamilyLife Publishing®
5800 Ranch Drive
Little Rock, Arkansas 72223
1-800-FL-TODAY · FamilyLife.com
FLTI, d/b/a FamilyLife®, is a ministry of Cru®

ISBN: 978-1-60200-915-8

Written by Shelby Abbott
Design: Jonathan Edwards

Printed in the United States of America

24 23 22 21 20   1 2 3 4 5
FAMILYLIFE˚

FOREWORD

As a pastor, I genuinely enjoy ministering to marriages and families. I remember when my wife and I lived together for a season before marriage, even though we felt conflicted. It was our struggles that cultivated a unique passion for cohabitating couples over the last twenty years. We are committed to helping cohabitating couples navigate the challenges of cohabitation.

Many cohabitating couples do not marry for a variety of reasons. A 2019 Pew Research Center survey indicates that more U.S. adults are delaying marriage—or foregoing it altogether. This research shows many find cohabitation acceptable, even for couples who do not plan to get married. It also denotes that a narrow majority says society is better off if couples in long-term relationships ultimately get married.

Our church has invested in ministering to cohabitating couples for the last ten years. We have helped over eighty cohabitating couples step into the covenant of marriage. One of the reasons I am so thankful for *What's the Point* is that it is a great book for assisting cohabitating couples.

What's the Point is an excellent resource in helping navigate this ever-changing landscape of cohabitation. This book is a tremendous resource for pastors, parents, marriage ministry leaders, counselors, college campus leaders, and those who need tools to assist couples considering marriage.

BRYAN CARTER,
Senior Pastor, Concord Church, Dallas, Texas

INTRODUCTION

They used to call it "shackin' up"—but is it really all about what our parents' generation thought: couch cuddles, sex with minimal effort, and no longer holding back the volume of your burps? Living together (cohabitating) as a romantic couple is commonplace in our culture. It's accepted as a natural "next step" for any dating couple once the relationship gets serious enough. It's viewed as a good idea, a test-drive to help you see if you should move from being boyfriend and girlfriend to being (gulp) spouses.

Moving in together instead of getting married is actually a relatively new thing. At the end of the 1960s, living with an unmarried partner didn't happen all that much; in fact, only 0.1 percent of 18- to 24-year olds lived with an unmarried partner. As of 2018, however, "15 percent of young adults live with an unmarried partner."[1] That's quite a drastic hike upward in fifty years.

So why the massive culture shift? Why have things changed so much in such a short period of time? Well, I believe there are several reasons, and not all of them have to do with combining incomes so a couple can afford more tacos every Tuesday. Nor is it just about sex. Maybe it was modeled for you. From your own upbringing, perhaps it was simply accepted that people live together without getting married. They may have acted as husband and wife without the official title and nobody in your family thought anything of it.

As we'll see in the coming chapters, there are several reasons why some couples decide to live together, and why others decide to wait until marriage before they move in with one another. My goal here will be to look at this subject matter from multiple angles and discuss obvious related topics like money and romance, but also more nuanced issues like spirituality, mental health, and stability. And since this topic touches on so much about the human experience, it matters that we look at it with scrutiny and sincerity. Lives can veer in one direction or the other based on choices made that are directly related to this issue. It matters that I study it, and it matters that you do too.

For the sake of clarity, I've divided the subject into two sections. In part one, we'll take a closer look at the topic of cohabitation, and in part two we'll ask the important question of "What's the point?" when it comes to marriage. My aim is to answer this question along with a few others that might be tumbling around in your brain concerning marriage and living together. Let's dive in.

PART ONE: LIVING TOGETHER

1

AN IMAGINARY SAFETY NET

When I was in third grade, I climbed a large pine tree in our backyard, found the sturdiest branch that could hold my weight without bending, and stood to my feet on the thickest part. I extended my arms straight out to my sides and started slowly walking away from the trunk, one foot in front of the other, as if I were on a tightrope under the circus big top.

This stunt didn't go well. I lost my balance, fell, and crashed hard on the grass below, leaving a large cut on my chin and knocking the wind out of me. Looking back, I'm glad I didn't climb much higher or something far worse could've happened to my fragile eight-year-old bones. "Ouch," I thought. "There's a reason high-wire entertainers use a safety net." Then I ran to my mom while crying.

Though you may never find yourself on the end of a tree branch, sometimes the uneasiness of life can leave you feeling as if you're walking a wire of your own. To combat these uncertainties, each of us often looks for "safety nets" that can provide cushions of security from potential disasters.

Things get particularly tricky, however, when it comes to the world of romantic relationships. If you really think about it, there aren't many safety nets when it comes to love. Putting yourself out there is scary, and despite the amazing picture you used for your dating profile, eventually there will be a face-to-face with the other person that exposes who you really are. Faces are seen in the flesh, social skills are put to the test, and conversation agility is evaluated. In the end, there's really not a lot of cushion.

In fact, a single buddy of mine recently told me he has nine dating apps on his phone—and uses every single one of them—but hasn't been on a real date in over two years. When I asked him why he hadn't gone out with somebody in all that time, he grunted, "Girls are scary, man."

Perhaps this is why there's such an affinity for something like moving in together. From the outside looking in, living with your partner can be seen as a safety net for marriage relationships under the belief that it affords couples the security of testing things out without the pressure of binding commitments. According to a recent article at the Institute for Family Studies, "Cohabitation is often viewed as a way to either strengthen a couple's bond or recognize incompatibilities—thus acting as a 'safety net' that might help prevent divorce."[2]

Logic would certainly seem to point us in the direction of opting for a cohabitation safety net because, as every romantic song out there tells us, love is hard. And many of us have seen the difficulty up close. My mom and dad divorced when I was four years old, and their relationship was awful. So even as a young kid, living together made sense to me. Sometimes bad marriages are all we see, and alternate routes seem smarter. It's been said that you can't aspire to what you don't know, and some of us simply weren't exposed to the idea that a happy, successful marriage is possible.

Consequently, it makes sense to try out living together for a while before getting married, right? You want to find out if you're compatible on a day-to-day basis, don't you? You want to see if you're able to bond with the other person when they're around you all the time; why is that a bad thing? You'd never buy a car without test-driving it, right?

These kinds of questions are valid and worth the time it takes to look into them because there seems to be an instinct within us that desires to experience love for a lifetime. And in the soil of that desire, these types of questions spring up.

Why? Because we care about love. Songs and movies about love relationships grip us in ways that other topics don't. Conversations about romance almost always capture our attention in a way that stirs our emotions and makes us long to be the center of someone else's affections. The choices we make in our quest for lifetime love, regardless of our rhetoric in the process, reveal what's going on in our hearts. So let's examine our options with intentionality.

WHAT THE RESEARCH SAYS

Cold, hard facts, while cold and also hard, are level playing ground for most people . . . except for the conspiracy theorists who believe there's an underground city below Denver International Airport that will house the New World Order after the apocalypse. In general, however, facts do the job of convincing the masses. So, what does the research tell us about living together and its ability to ward off future relationship problems or divorce? The results may surprise you.

"Research has consistently shown that the cords of the cohabitation 'safety net' do not hold up under pressure, nor do they typically last long term."[3] Of all the studies that have been done with couples who live together, the facts have communicated over and over again that cohabitation before marriage actually puts couples at an increased risk of getting a divorce one day. I know that may sound counterintuitive, but according to Michael J. Rosenfeld and Katharina Roesler of the *Journal of Marriage and Family*, it's the truth.

Before any of the data existed on premarital cohabitation, scholars assumed it would lead to lower rates of divorce. But once the research was done and the data flooded in, Rosenfeld and Roesler found that living together before getting married was directly associated with just the opposite: "higher divorce rates."[4]

The cost for living together is far greater when you consider the long-term outcome of marital disillusionment over the temporary happiness of being under the same roof before officially committing to one another. Not to mention that one of the nation's foremost experts in this area states that living together has been "consistently associated with poorer marital communication quality, lower marital satisfaction, [and] higher levels of domestic violence."[5]

COHABITATION BEFORE MARRIAGE ACTUALLY PUTS COUPLES AT AN INCREASED RISK OF GETTING A DIVORCE ONE DAY.

So why the massive disconnect between the assumed benefits and glaring reality? Undoubtedly, there are several reasons, but one of the major elements to blame is communication or, more precisely, the lack of communication.

SLIDING, NOT DECIDING

Carla, a friend of mine from high school, has lived with five different men since she was eighteen. Now, in her late thirties and living on her own, Carla says she always expected the relationship she was in at the time to go a certain way, but it never did. She'd get swept up in the excitement of it all and never really talk about what her hopes and dreams were with her boyfriend . . . only to find herself let down when the inevitable breakup would come.

Someone very wise once told me, "Disappointment comes from unmet expectations," and I think that's at the heart of what we're talking about here. Many young men and women assume that living together is the next step to take when a romantic relationship gets more serious, and consequently they never really talk about it.

"It sort of just happened," is what you will often hear from couples who live together without getting married. It's much more of a quick decision to move in together because there's less of a commitment; and if it doesn't work out, there's a quick exit. This is what research professor Scott Stanley calls "sliding versus deciding," and what one journalist describes as, "a gradual slope, one not marked by rings or ceremonies or sometimes even a conversation. Couples bypass talking about why they want to live together and what it will mean."[6]

Research has found that partners often have different, unspoken agendas, combined with an assumption that the other person is thinking they're moving in together for the same reasons. However, because of gender asymmetry, this often isn't the reality of the motivation behind a decision to cohabitate. Meg Jay of the *New York Times* says, "Women are more likely to view cohabitation as a step toward marriage, while men are more likely to see it as a way to test a relationship or postpone commitment."[7] The man thinks one thing; the woman thinks another. Neither of them has an intentional conversation about why they're moving in together, and life certainly seems easier under the same roof, so it just happens. Sliding, not deciding.

"COUPLES BYPASS TALKING ABOUT WHY THEY WANT TO LIVE TOGETHER AND WHAT IT WILL MEAN."

Without being intentional about such a decision, many can look around and feel stuck instead of liberated by the so-called safety net of cohabitation. Why? Because sliding into living together is easy, but sliding out is not. Jay illustrates this nicely when she writes, "Too often, young adults enter into what they imagine will be low-cost, low-risk living situations only to find themselves unable to get out months, even years, later.

"COHABITATION IS LOADED WITH SETUP AND SWITCHING COSTS."

It's like signing up for a credit card with 0 percent interest. At the end of 12 months when the interest goes up to 23 percent you feel stuck because your balance is too high to pay off. In fact, cohabitation can be exactly like that.

"In behavioral economics, it's called consumer lock-in. Lock-in is the decreased likelihood to search for, or change to, another option once an investment in something has been made. The greater the setup costs, the less likely we are to move to another, even better, situation, especially when faced with switching costs, or the time, money and effort it requires to make a change."

Jay goes on to note, "Cohabitation is loaded with setup and switching costs. Living together can be . . . economical, and the setup costs are subtly woven in. After years of living among roommates' junky old stuff, couples happily split the rent on a nice one-bedroom apartment. They share wireless and pets and enjoy shopping for new furniture together. Later, these setup and switching costs have an impact on how likely they are to leave."[8]

It would seem that many opt for the path of least resistance if they're feeling the tug to move on or break up with the person they're living with. They just don't want the obvious hassle or relational dissonance. Sliding out comes with a lot of problematic circumstances or awkwardness, so they stay. What once seemed like liberating and easy cohabitation has now turned into a feeling of being trapped.

A few months ago, I asked my friend Lauren why she was still living with Lucas after admitting to me that she didn't love him anymore. "There's just too much wrapped up in him right now and, frankly, without his paycheck, I couldn't afford to keep the electricity on in our house, let alone feed my kids."

Lauren has two kids from a previous boyfriend, and when she moved in with Lucas, it seemed like the best thing for everyone involved . . . plus she was caught up with the romantic emotion of it all and excited to have someone in her life again. But now the romance has soured with Lucas, and Lauren feels trapped in what she calls a "loveless, sexless, communication-less relationship with a man who simply pays the bills."

MORE PROBLEMS

As much as you'd like to think the safety net of living together will save you from heartache both in the present and the future, the statistics prove otherwise. "Not only does cohabitation fail as a divorce-prevention safety net, it may also be associated with increased marital infidelity."[9]

In fact, according to an iFidelity survey funded by the Wheatley Institution and conducted by YouGov, "Those who had cohabited two or more times in their life before marriage were 15 percentage points more likely to have been either emotionally, sexually, or electronically unfaithful to their spouse than those who did not cohabit."[10]

Why is this? It would seem that what people believe the safety net of cohabitation to be simply doesn't exist in the real world. It's imaginary. It doesn't provide the security of testing things out without the pressure of the "binding" commitment of marriage.

It's not the safety net to prevent divorce. In fact, it's just the opposite.

Living together brings present problems and more drastic future ones too. And as we'll continue to see in the coming chapters, it isn't all it's cracked up to be.

AN IMAGINARY SAFETY NET-

1. Why do you think living together is so appealing to many couples?

2. How does the research that's been done on co-habitation shift your perspective (if at all) on the attractive nature of living together?

3. How do you think you'd feel if you were stuck in a cohabiting situation that you simply couldn't slide out of without major problems?

2

THE MYTH OF
MORE MONEY

One plus one doesn't always add up to two—
when the variable of humanity is thrown into the
equation. You would assume that if two people
who had separate incomes decided to move in
together, the household would collectively benefit as a whole. One income from her plus one
income from him equals two combined incomes

for more overall cash flow at home. Makes sense, right? Well once again, the research shows otherwise.

Writer and director of family formation studies at Focus on the Family, Glenn T. Stanton observes, "Only 4 percent of homes with a married mother and father are on food stamps at any given time. But 21 percent of cohabiting . . . homes require such public assistance."[11]

What is this saying? For whatever reason, cohabiting homes as opposed to married homes are significantly more prone to poverty. In fact, Stanton goes on to say, "marital status has increasingly become the central factor in whether [people] rise above, remain, or descend into poverty."[12]

Cohabiting people, regardless of how much money they have, tend to manage their funds differently than married people. It comes in at the same speed of the average married person but goes out at a much quicker rate. And the reasons as to why this happens aren't terribly perplexing. Spending, rather than saving, is the common default setting if a person isn't married, and couples who simply live together seem to amount to a pair of spenders under the same roof instead of a committed married couple planning and saving for the future.

An unmarried friend of mine named Kevin once came to me and complained about not having enough money to start saving for the future. Kevin was in his mid-twenties at the time, and I asked him a few clarifying questions as to what he meant. He said that with his salary, he couldn't invest or put any money away because he didn't make enough. I told him that when I was in my mid-twenties, I was making $19,000 a year, but I was still able to put $200 per month into mutual funds. With his mouth slightly agape, he uttered, "How?"

I told him I made intentional choices when it came to my budget, and there were some places I made sacrifices. After going over some of the rough numbers of where Kevin was spending his money, we discovered he was spending way too much money on going out to eat. Rarely did he cook a meal at home or pack a lunch for work, so with a few adjustments, we were able to find money in his monthly budget to invest.

COHABITING COUPLES CAN EASILY BECOME BLIND TO HOW MUCH MONEY THEY ARE ACTUALLY SPENDING . . .

Stories like Kevin's aren't unusual. And if a man with an aloof attitude toward money ends up moving in with a woman with a similar attitude—carefree about where her dollars go—the combination can lead to serious problems. Incorporate that with dinner dates at a restaurant, entertainment expenses, stay-in streaming services, gifts, new furniture, etc., and the bills start to pile up quickly. Cohabiting couples can easily become blind to how much money they are actually spending on a day-to-day basis and, therefore, save less for the future or for an emergency situation.

APPLIANCE DEATH

When my wife and I had been married for a little over two years, we purchased a single-family ranch home where we knew we wanted to settle for the foreseeable future. To our delight, we were able to negotiate all of the major appliances of the house into the contract, so we wouldn't have to buy a bunch of expensive devices immediately after signing a mortgage. All was well in our new home until about three months after we moved in and the appliances started to fail.

The refrigerator died first, followed quickly by both the washer and the dryer. Then the lawn mower, then the dishwasher, and finally the furnace and air conditioner. Yep, all of them kicked the bucket within the first year of buying our home, and to replace them all was—how should I say this?—not cheap.

By the grace of God, we started saving money in an emergency fund as soon as we were married two years previously, so we were able to pay cash to replace our broken down appliances and not go into debt.

I've found that not many people think too far ahead for situations like the one I just described unless they make a commitment to their significant other. Few couples who decide to live together think through the potential financial pitfalls of something like appliance death when they move in together, and this is what I'm getting at.

Now, can a cohabiting couple save up for emergencies and set a budget to make sure they know where their money is going? Of course. I'm not saying it's impossible to have an emergency fund if you're living with your partner and unmarried.

What I am saying, however, is that because there is less emphasis placed on commitment to each other, each partner in a cohabiting pair has a tendency to think of the money they make as *their* money, not *our* money. This is normal, and I'm not slamming it, but you can see how this can lead to potential difficulties when couple-type problems need to be solved by cohabitors with individual incomes.

MONEY PITFALLS

If you open up nearly any premarital counseling book, you'll probably find at least one chapter, if not several, on money and budgeting. Why? Because money is almost always a complicated subject.

Everyone is raised in a way in which they take a certain approach toward finances. Some families are spontaneous with how they spend their money; some are quite strict when it comes to spending. Some people are very interested in monitoring investments and savings, and some are in the habit of hiding their valuables in obscure places. Many are raised in virtual poverty with no such thing as an emergency fund, while others are born with the proverbial silver spoon in their mouths and never want for anything. There's no one way people approach money, and we tend to mimic what we learn as we grow up.

> **EACH PARTNER IN A COHABITING PAIR HAS A TENDENCY TO THINK OF THE MONEY THEY MAKE AS *THEIR* MONEY, NOT *OUR* MONEY.**

For example, my parents are more spontaneous spenders, and that has rubbed off on me. If I walk into Target and see something I'd like to purchase (whether it be a picture frame or masculine loofa), I usually get it.

My wife, however, was raised in an environment where her dad was extremely careful about spending and much more interested in saving and investing.

And because my wife and I don't make much money in our professions, she's extremely frugal and financially cautious—the opposite of impulsive.

Naturally, we've had a lot of heated conversations when it comes to the budget. But we're married, committed to each other and working things out in the best ways for our family, so we make it work. My educated guess would be that money problems can cause serious damage to cohabiting relationships where there's no commitment to marriage. It's already difficult as it is when a couple is married.

WEALTH-GENERATING INSTITUTION

The scholars at the National Marriage Project working from the University of Virginia explain that marriage itself is a "wealth-generating institution.[13] Stanton expounds, "Marriage generates wealth largely because marriage molds men into producers, providers, and savers. Singleness and cohabiting don't. . . . Nobel-winning economist George Akerlof explains this is because 'men settle down when they get married and if they fail to get married, they fail to settle down.'

"This is precisely why every insurance company offers lower premiums on health and auto insurance to married men. Settled-down men also work more, earn more, save more, and spend more money on their families than on themselves. They boost the well-being of women and children in every important way."[14]

Conversely, when a man moves in with his girlfriend, he is likely to spend his money in the way he wants to spend it; and that usually means he spends it on himself. This isn't true of every guy in this category, but in general, he isn't totally "settled down" when he's living with his girlfriend because an official commitment to her hasn't been made.

So one income plus one income in cohabitation under the same roof doesn't necessarily add up to two collective incomes. The idea that you'll have more money if you're living with your boyfriend or girlfriend is a myth, because research shows that married people consistently rate better in the area of income.

THE MYTH OF MORE MONEY-

1. Why do you think the topic of money is such a complicated subject for so many couples (either married or cohabiting)?

2. In what ways are you surprised by the research stating that couples who simply live together have less money than their married peers?

3. How can a married man boost the well-being of a woman in ways a cohabiting man cannot?

3

A LACK OF
SATISFACTION

I've told myself many times that I need to stop reading online reviews of movies before I see them. I've lost count of how many times my anticipation for a film was super high because of positive digital chatter, followed by a looming sense of disappointment when the two-hour flick didn't live up to the hype. I'm starting to believe movie reviews are just clickbait.

When my expectations don't get met, my experience is overwhelmed by a lack of satisfaction. Likewise, I'm persuaded that the expectations surrounding what someone believes will happen when living together generates a lack of satisfaction too. Meg Jay from the *New York Times* observes, "Couples who cohabit before marriage (and especially before an engagement or an otherwise clear commitment) tend to be less satisfied with their marriages—and more likely to divorce—than couples who do not."

Jay continues, "Research suggests that serial cohabitators [those who have moved in with their boyfriend or girlfriend more than once], couples with differing levels of commitment, and those who use cohabitation as a test are most at risk for poor relationship quality and eventual relationship dissolution."[15]

I'm reminded of a story about a woman named Kaylee. When Kaylee graduated from college, she and her boyfriend of two years moved into an apartment together near their jobs. At first, everything was exciting as they shopped for furniture together at IKEA, spent lots of time with each other, and even bought a dog together.

Kaylee and her boyfriend, Adam, lived together for five years and finally got married as they both approached their thirties. Sadly, less than a year after the wedding, Kaylee was looking for a divorce lawyer and wondering how it all went wrong. She shared that she never felt like Adam was ever truly committed to her, and that living together felt like she was on a five-year, never-ending audition to be his wife. And about a year after her divorce from Adam, Kaylee moved in with her new boyfriend, Joel, no doubt expecting this relationship to go better.

THE FORMULA DOESN'T WORK

The all-too-common formula of dating, then living together, then (maybe) marrying just doesn't work when it comes to satisfaction. Meg Jay explains, "I've had other clients who also wish they hadn't sunk years of their twenties into relationships that would have lasted only months had they not been living together. Others want to feel committed to their partners, yet they are confused about whether they have consciously chosen their mates. Founding relationships on convenience or ambiguity can interfere with the process of claiming the people we love. A life built on top of 'maybe you'll do' simply may not feel as dedicated as a life built on top of the 'we do' of commitment or marriage."[16]

We've already seen in chapter one how cohabitation fails to work as a divorce-prevention safety net, but not many assume it will ultimately fail to provide a couple with the kind of satisfaction they crave from a romantic relationship as well. It's a shame we can't see that.

There are many mistakes in my past I wish I could go back and fix: fashion choices in the early 2000s, the hot dog I ate at that minor league baseball game, and dating the girl whose father was a professional arm wrestler (for real). But in comparison to the blunder of moving in with the wrong person for an extended season, the errors I mentioned feel relatively small. Why? Because moving in with your boyfriend or girlfriend actually *increases* your chances of what one author calls "spending too much time on a mistake."[17]

No one on their deathbed wishes they had spent more time with the wrong people. And if that's the case, why even risk it? Moving in with someone is not a step toward, or even a convenient test for, a long-lasting, satisfying relationship. Many find the whole experience to be a proverbial sugar-substitute when it comes to relationship needs. It does not gratify the longings we have for authentic connection and commitment with another person, because that's something only a marriage relationship can do.

"FOUNDING RELATIONSHIPS ON CONVENIENCE OR AMBIGUITY CAN INTERFERE WITH THE PROCESS OF CLAIMING THE PEOPLE WE LOVE. A LIFE BUILT ON TOP OF 'MAYBE YOU'LL DO' SIMPLY MAY NOT FEEL AS DEDICATED AS A LIFE BUILT ON TOP OF THE 'WE DO' OF COMMITMENT OR MARRIAGE."

COMMUNICATION WOES

There have been many young couples who have allowed life "to just happen" to them instead of living with intentionality and purposeful pursuit. For example, we mentioned in chapter one the "sliding, not deciding" concept many couples adopt that ultimately ends up leaving them feeling trapped in the relationship. However, if a couple were open, vulnerable, and willing to lean into the tough conversations, there would be no sliding.

I'd argue that healthy, clear communication is the antidote to a large percentage of problems in any given romantic relationship. When couples reject the communication status quo they adopted when they were in early high school and grow into a more robust, mature form of communication, many satisfying results occur.

For example, they don't play relationship games with each other. When I say games, I'm not referring to busting out Monopoly on a Saturday night and enjoying a little healthy competition. I mean the specific scheming that can go on between a couple in an attempt to elicit a certain response from their partner. It's essentially intentional manipulation for the purposes of either getting what they want, subtly asserting dominance, or triggering that unexplained jolt of adrenaline one gets when he or she tampers with someone's emotions and their heart is on the line.

Relationship games are carefully crafted manifestations of selfishness, and they do nothing but hurt other people. Women say one thing but mean another. Men will act a certain way one evening but then act another way the next day. She will send a cryptic text to see how he'll respond. He will act interested in another girl just to make her jealous. You know, juvenile stuff.

> **HEALTHY, CLEAR COMMUNICATION IS THE ANTIDOTE TO A LARGE PERCENTAGE OF PROBLEMS IN ANY GIVEN ROMANTIC RELATIONSHIP.**

There's this verse in the Bible that says, "When I was a child, I spoke like a child, I thought like a child, I reasoned like a child. When I became a man, I gave up childish ways."[18] Gut punch, huh? But what is this saying to us today?

Probably something like this: little boys and little girls send mixed messages that are supposed to "mean something." But when little boys and little girls become men and women, they give up childish ways and communicate with one another. When we are clear about our intentions and uninterested in messing around with another person's heart, roads are opened toward vulnerability, trust, honesty, and eventually a strong bond.

MAYBE IT'S TIME WE FOUGHT FOR OUR RELATIONSHIPS IN A WAY THAT DOESN'T TAKE THE PATH OF LEAST RESISTANCE AS COHABITATION DOES.

There's a strong dissatisfaction in the hearts of many young couples who cohabitate because they slide into living together, then slide into decisions and habits while really never talking about them first. They do life alongside each other and never communicate on a deeper level. They get insecure about the nature of the other's commitment, so they start to play relationship games and do and say hurtful things. They manipulate to get a response out of their partner, all the while longing to be truly known in a way that simply living together will never provide.

A BETTER WAY?

Perhaps there's a better way. A better plan. A better relationship DNA that encourages more mature romantic relationships. Maybe it's time we fought for our relationships in a way that doesn't take the path of least resistance as cohabitation does.

If you want to get a job somewhere, you don't just walk into the lobby and lounge around in your sweatpants, waiting for someone to walk up to you and offer you a position at the company. No, you work on your resumé, you fill out a job application, you set up an interview, you buy the appropriate business attire and get cleaned up. You remind yourself to keep eye contact and sit up straight when you're being evaluated by the boss, and you do whatever it takes to get that job offer.[19]

How much more important is your relationship than a job offer? If you're committed to traveling the best road—not the easiest—toward a fulfilling romantic relationship, it will most certainly be worth your effort. I'm not guaranteeing a perfect romance, but

I can say that even when a relationship doesn't work out, it would be healthy to look back on it without the shame that often comes with doing what was easiest at the time.

Moving in together is easy. And as we've seen, it isn't ultimately satisfying. But there is another road to take. There is another option. There is another paradigm to think through when it comes to your romantic life. We'll examine that alternate road in the second section.

A LACK OF SATISFACTION-

1. When it comes to a romantic relationship, have you ever "spent too much time on a mistake"? What ultimately made you get out of that relationship?

2. Why do you think cohabitation is unsatisfying to so many couples?

3. Why do you think we are often fine with the lack of effort we put into our relationships and "sliding" into them? How does cohabitation encourage the "sliding effect"?

PART
TWO: AN
ALTERNATE
ROUTE

4

WHY MARRIAGE?

There are many things people search for in order to gain a deeper sense of purpose and meaning, and I believe one of the most significant is marriage.

Marriage is kind of like the northern lights. I can describe to you in great detail what it's like to see the northern lights in person: it covers the entire night sky, it's full of amazing movement and color, it's beautiful and breathtaking. But to really know what it's like, you have to be there.

Similarly, I can describe to you some of the wonderful things about being married: the companionship, the intimacy, the trust, the laughter and fun, the joy of seeing your children grow and learn. But if you really want to know the benefits of marriage, you have to be there.

That being said, I want to do my best here to paint a vivid picture that stirs a longing within you for marriage. There are a remarkable amount of reasons why a couple should pursue getting married instead of simply moving in together, and while I certainly can't cover *every* reason here in this little book, I'll try to give you three compelling reasons as you ask sincere questions like, "What's the meaning of marriage?" and "Why should we bother with such a commitment when cohabitation seems so much easier?"

CLOSER RELATIONSHIP

Journalist Maggie Gallagher once observed, "Married people are both responsible for and responsible to another human being, and both halves of that dynamic lead the married to live more responsible, fruitful, and satisfying lives. Marriage is a transformative act, changing the way two people look at each other, at the future, and at their roles in society."[20]

Naturally, when you commit to another person as a spouse, the commitment lays a foundation for a deep connection with them in a way that can't be replicated. A bond forms between the married couple and becomes that "transformative act" turning the two people into one, much like an alloy.

An alloy is a metal made by combining two metallic elements, giving it greater strength and resistance to corrosion. The combination as a whole is greater than its individual parts. Why? Because they are better than the simple sum of one plus one. They are blended together into something new and bonded in a way that simple, everyday proximity can't replicate. Marriage brings a closeness unlike any other relationship a person can have, and positively changes not only the couple who is married, but the society they are a part of as well.

Now, I know this isn't true for everybody as if marriage were some magic spell that cured all of our companionship issues and friendship woes. In fact, my parents are anything but friends now because divorce has a way of interfering with a couple's friendship. Being married certainly doesn't guarantee close companionship, however, marriage has a far better track record at creating a closeness than cohabitation ever will.

NO OTHER RELATIONSHIP I HAVE IS LIKE THE ONE I HAVE WITH MY WIFE . . .

That being said (and I know this sounds cliché), I consider my wife to be my best friend. The blessing of getting to spend my life with someone I really love but also really *like* is a total win. And each year that goes by, I feel like we get closer and closer in a way that makes the previous year pale by comparison. Our friendship has the perfect opportunity to grow as time moves forward because it's rooted in the perfect environment: our marriage. No other relationship I have is like the one I have with my wife, and its uniqueness is what makes it so precious.

BETTER SEX

We were destined to get to this subject at some point, and here we are. Let me start by saying something that might be a bit of a surprise to you: married people have better sex, and they have it more often. Why? Well, Gallagher says, "Despite the lurid . . . marketing that promises singles erotic joys untold, both husbands and wives are more likely to report that they have an extremely satisfying sex life than are singles or cohabitors."[21]

Let me explain what I mean here without using a sexual metaphor. (I know you must be thinking, *Thank God!*) When a bond is made via a sexual experience, it is not something that can be easily removed. Engaging in a sexual act with another person is meant to exist within a committed marriage relationship, and without that proper context, lives can quickly be destroyed. Why? Because it's *important*. Even the popular British band, The 1975, in their song "Somebody Else" considers sex to be more like "intertwining your soul" with another person as opposed to the simple physical act itself. As a secular band, their song would seem to indicate they see the meaningful significance of sex (well, maybe).

However, our modern cultural perspective would have you believe that sex is just a thing that happens between two people for the purpose of experiencing selfish pleasure. Even the phrase "get some" is intrinsically self-serving. This perspective treats the act of sex like the random placement of a sticky note to any person you want to "get some" from. Stick to someone here, then peel away. If you like that person, stick to them for a bit, then peel away. Stick to the hot person you met at the bar, then peel away in the morning. Stick to the person you've had a crush on, then peel away. Be a sticky note.

But the catch is, sex is not a temporary thing. It's a bond between a man and woman in a loving, committed marriage that is intended to build a stronger relationship over time. Sex is not like a sticky note, it's more like an envelope. Ugh, I know I'm talking a lot about paper products here, but stay with me.

When a sexual attachment is made between two

people, it's like an envelope flap being sealed at the opening for the purpose of creating a secure bond. And we all know what happens when an envelope is opened, right? There is permanent damage done when the ripping apart starts. Even though they are somewhat obsolete in our digital age, have you ever tried to use an envelope again after it's been sealed and then reopened? It's kind of pointless to try, isn't it? Why? Because it was meant to be attached only one time.

The modern cultural perspective would have you believe that sex should be treated as if everyone in the world is a sticky note, but what happens to a sticky note if you stick it on too many things? It eventually loses its stickiness,

> **SEX IS NOT A TEMPORARY THING. IT'S A BOND BETWEEN A MAN AND WOMAN IN A LOVING, COMMITTED MARRIAGE THAT IS INTENDED TO BUILD A STRONGER RELATIONSHIP OVER TIME.**

doesn't it? Sex is not a sticky note-type scenario; it's more like an envelope, meant to be attached once, without being pulled apart and causing irreparable damage.[22]

As a married man, I can honestly say there has never been a time in my marriage when I've thought to myself, "I really wish that I had done more sexually before I got married." And I have certainly never thought, "I wish that my wife had more experience in the bedroom before she married me."

But don't just take my word for it. The research aligns with what I'm telling you. Gallagher states, "Married people are also the most likely to report a highly satisfying sex life. Wives, for example, are almost twice as likely as divorced and never-married women to have a sex life that (a) exists and (b) is extremely satisfying emotionally. Contrary to popular lore, for men, having a wife beats shacking up by a wide margin: 50 percent of husbands say sex with their partner is extremely satisfying physically, compared with 39 percent of cohabiting men."[23]

More satisfying and more frequent sex? Marriage has perks.

KIDS MAKE YOU STRONGER

True, there are loads of people who live together and

have kids, so why would I say "kids make you stronger" as a good reason for marriage? Well, it comes back again to the issue of commitment. As it turns out, there is a huge difference between having children as a married couple and having children as a couple who only lives together.

Casey Leins of *U.S. News and World Report* says, "Many of these cohabiting couples are also having children, half of the time unintentionally, according to data from 1982 to 2010 that was used in the [National Health Statistics Report]. Without the many advantages of marriage, including significant eco-nomic benefits and social support systems, it's likely that the stress and responsibility of raising a child can contribute to a relationship's demise. This idea is supported by the fact that, when an unmarried couple lives together and has a baby, there is only a 20 percent chance they will be married by the child's 5th birthday."[24]

Okay, so if I'm married with kids, how does that make me stronger? Well, think about it this way: a bicep muscle gets bigger and stronger by working it out. In other words, a muscle needs to be broken down in order to be built back up. And the same goes for our overall character and temperament in life.

One of my favorite things about being alive is the fact that I'm a dad of two girls. My children are delightful in ways I never thought possible. That being said, raising children certainly has a way of helping me come face-to-face with my preexisting selfish disposition. But as difficult as it is, I'm better for it. There are no shortcuts on the road to character, and to be a parent is to sacrifice. Sometimes rewards come through the medium of sacrifice. In fact, there are certain kinds of rewards that *only* come about that way.

When you love someone, you give of yourself so that they might benefit; and that, by definition, is sacrifice. Many of us look at parents with screaming kids in the fit of a tantrum at the grocery store and think, "I'm glad I'm not that parent." But in reality, when parental self-sacrifice is ushered into our lives so that we might be part of shepherding the soul of a child, I believe it is increasing our kindness and compassion. It's helping us grow.

I once met this couple in a coffee shop who looked like they were in their late forties or early fifties. When I sat down near them, we struck up a conversation and I immediately noticed that both the husband and the wife didn't put up with inconveniences too well. She complained about the residual sugar crystals and wet coffee cup circles on her table as she wiped them up with a disposable wet cloth she pulled from her purse. He got flustered when his white shoe rubbed up against the table leg and got scuffed, and both of them couldn't stop staring daggers at the baby in the highchair a few tables away who, according to them, "Just would not . . . Shut. Up."

WHEN YOU LOVE SOMEONE, YOU GIVE OF YOURSELF SO THAT THEY MIGHT BENEFIT; AND THAT, BY DEFINITION, IS SACRIFICE.

I asked them how long they had been married, and they answered, "Twenty-two years." I then asked if they had kids, and they both said in unison, "Nope."

Their coffee-shop demeanor suddenly made sense to me. Raising kids has a way of making a man and a woman stronger and less intolerant of life's little annoyances. Why? Because sacrificing forces you to see life from a perspective that's uncomfortable. It makes you adjust, move, rethink, and grow. It helps you adapt and prepares you for the inevitable messiness of life.

Marriage is a place where grown-ups do the tough work of helping children mature into adults . . . and adults put away childish behavior. Giving of yourself as a parent is the breaking down and building back up of you as a person. You become the better for it because you become a better human being. If that's not a solid reason to consider marriage instead of living together, I don't know what is.

––––––––––––

Again, there are many more reasons to pursue marriage, but hopefully only giving you three in this chapter will whet your appetite to look for more. As you examine the merits of marriage, I think it will be much easier to put cohabitation on trial in the courtroom of your mind and ask it the all-too-important question, "What's the point?"

In fact, if you believe in the Creator or Originator, there's an even more compelling reason why marriage is the best place to experience what our lives were ultimately made for. It actually seems like the point of marriage was created to point us to a bigger story. A love story all of us were designed to experience.

WHY MARRIAGE?-

1. In what ways can you see marriage bringing you closer to someone than you've ever been with another person?

2. Have you ever considered that sex is better inside the context of marriage? How has your paradigm changed (if at all) after reading this chapter?

3. How is self-sacrifice a means to becoming a better person? What does that have to do with raising children as a married person?

5

THE POINT

Be true to yourself. Although we've heard this message in nearly every Disney movie over the last several decades, it's actually a terrible piece of advice. What part of myself am I supposed to be true to? If I look down into the depths of who I am, I don't always like what I find there. I, like most people, am conflicted and often wrestle with myself on the inside.

In reality, people who give this kind of advice know deep down that it's not true. What if a guy is "being true to himself" but he's a complete jerk? What if he says that he's being true to his authentic identity, but he's a bigot, or a terrorist, or a rapist, or a murderer? Each of us would probably admit that he doesn't have a good identity to be true to in the first place.

There's much better counsel to people than simply "find your true self" when we all know that true self may not be worth following.[25]

I'm convinced that we all need something more significant than platitudes such as this if we're going to thrive as human beings. Let's look at marriage through the lens of a specific perspective and then examine what I like to call the "ultimate marriage" that leads to thriving, abundant life.

SPIRITUAL SATISFACTION

I want to begin by saying that marriage can be satisfying not only in the ways we've already covered, but it can be spiritually satisfying as well. When a married couple is on the same page in relation to their perspectives about God, the Bible, and something like corporate worship at the same local church, that kind of alignment will unite them in ways that go much deeper than the physical, emotional, or even psychological connections.

How do I know this? Well, not only do I have this kind of connection personally with my wife, but I've seen what it's like when that connection doesn't exist. I've worked with college students for over twenty years and have had many conversations with young people who experience the pain of their significant other being on a different spiritual page.

Now, can a married couple be in disagreement about issues of spirituality too? Of course. But when the commitment of marriage exists in a relationship, the couple is much more likely to align to the same belief system. When you dig down into it, there should be nothing casual when it comes to your beliefs about God, and if there's a misalignment between a husband and wife in that area, it can't be brushed aside as if they are cheering for two different NFL teams. That spiritual issue quickly becomes *the* issue due to the fact that they *are* married. Rarely does a dating or cohabiting couple stay together when their lives don't line up spiritually, nor should they. Spiritual beliefs tap into the most important part of our lives; and when there isn't commonality between a couple there, it's simply not a good match.

Marriage is a profoundly enriching spiritual experience. Because of my wife, I have grown in my relationship with God, been challenged by her in ways that have made me more spiritually mature, been kept accountable to important spiritual disciplines that might have otherwise slipped out of my life, plus benefited in countless other ways—more than I can list here—and all under the banner of commitment to our marriage. I know that she's not going anywhere, and she knows I'm not leaving either—no matter what.

The spiritual nourishment we help provide to one another because of our commitment is priceless. And when times get tough (not *if*, but *when*), we'll have each other's backs when we need to be spiritually propped up. What a great picture, symbolizing our urgency for rescue and the ensuing harbor of relief and encouragement. Marriage is a way bigger deal than what some people refer to as "just a piece of paper saying we love each other."

Marriage is the arena God designed to reflect a relationship involving unconditional love, self-sacrifice, and unparalleled satisfying depth. It's the place where couples can model the fascinating oneness of God to each other and the world around them in a very specific way. It's a picture of what the Bible refers to as "the gospel"—in other words, the point.

THE ULTIMATE MARRIAGE

When most people get involved with another person romantically, they aren't intrinsically thinking, "It would be really great to be with this person so I can serve them sacrificially." We simply aren't wired that way because the undercurrent in every human heart is selfishness. Our flawed nature makes it nearly impossible to push *service* to the front of the line when it comes to main motivations for romance.

We typically view romantic relationships through

the lens of "What can they do for me? How will they make me feel? What will they do to serve me? How will they help improve my reputation? In what ways will they satisfy me and my cravings?"

Me. Me. Me. When it comes to romance, we are takers.

But what if the ultimate marriage isn't primarily about us and our selfish desires? What if we were in a different kind of relationship with someone who wasn't a taker but a giver? Someone who thought through the lens of "I can do this for you. I can make you feel loved. I can serve you. I will give to you. I can satisfy you." Sound perfect? Well, He is.

ME. ME. ME. WHEN IT COMES TO ROMANCE, WE ARE TAKERS.

We human beings think we know what is best for us, and that is why we are born to be rebels. All of us turn our backs on God and go our own way because we think we've got it all figured out. We substitute purity for poison and drink deeply from the unwashed cup it rests in. We are in need of rescue.

And although we are condemned to separation from God because of our rebellion, He still chooses to move toward us by absorbing the deserved punishment Himself in the person of Jesus Christ. The solution has presented itself quite clearly, and every person in the world is faced with a choice: personally receive the punishment for our own defiance or let Him take it. Either way, the price has to be paid.

Those who humble themselves and accept the gift God offers become what the Bible refers to as the bride of Christ (2 Corinthians 11:2; Ephesians 5:21-27; Revelation 21:1-2), and they no longer bear the burden of disapproval or judgment (Romans 8:1). They have experienced rescue.

But the incredible reward God offers in Jesus is not just a ticket to glory; it is the beginning of a relationship unlike any other. It is a personal relationship with our Maker, built upon true love, trust, intimacy, tenderness, and care. Eternity with God begins the day we make the decision to receive what He has offered. And when we take it, He begins the good work of healing us from within so we aren't just takers. Then, and only then, are we able to live a life characterized by love, because the foundation is solid.

Jesus is in the business of changing lives. He always has been, and He can do the good work of transforming you to be more like Him, despite the run-ins you will undoubtedly have with life's crazy relationships. All you have to do is ask Him to get involved and trust He'll follow through with His promises.

He will.

This is the good news that dramatically alters the way we view not only our eternal future but also our present struggles. In the midst of the pressures that will inevitably come our way, we can choose to lean into Christ's power over failure and death (Romans 6:1-11), instead of fleeing toward the escapism of our vices.

People who say yes to the payment made for them by Christ are God's people—Christians. Christians are the bride of Christ, and Jesus Christ is the bridegroom. I know it can be kind of tricky and weird to understand with this kind of marriage language that's used, but it's also beautiful when you think about it. One author explains, "With Christ's life, death on the cross, and resurrection, Jesus became the living embodiment of the bridegroom and a faithful husband who was willing to give up His life for the one He loved."[26]

The Groom dies for His bride. He intentionally lays down His life for the one He's devoted to. And He doesn't just die, He comes back to life and conquers death so the bride doesn't have to die herself. What's more romantic than that?

IN THE MIDST OF THE PRESSURES THAT WILL INEVITABLY COME OUR WAY, WE CAN CHOOSE TO LEAN INTO CHRIST'S POWER . . .

Wouldn't you want to do anything for the perfect person who willingly dies in your place and then comes back to life? Wouldn't that person be worthy of your allegiance, especially knowing that He holds the keys to life and death? That's a romance story I'd want to be a part of. That's a romance story I *am* a part of—as a Christian.

You can experience that romance too by saying "I do" to the perfect person who died so you could live. That is the way to step into the ultimate marriage with complete trust, security, love, acceptance, and joy.

Earthly marriage is meant to be a reflection of the heavenly marriage Christians experience with Jesus Christ. Of course, human beings are imperfect so the reflection isn't always the greatest, but living in the freedom of knowing that Christ died for my imperfect earthly marriage makes me love Him and my wife all the more.

My marriage to my wife is a symbol of the ultimate relationship I have that's infinitely more substantial. This is the point of marriage, put in place by the God of the universe, and He offers us as human beings the opportunity to participate in such a beautiful institution. Being in relationship with Him is thriving, abundant life, exposing platitudes like *be true to yourself* for what they really are: hollow.

If anything in this chapter has captured your attention, I want you to know that EveryPerson.com provides an extensive amount of content on the subject of knowing God personally, and serves as a safe place for the curious to ask questions/seek answers.

1. What do you think it looks like for a person to live based on something other than themselves and their own desires?

2. How can marriage lead to mutual spiritual satisfaction between a couple in a way that cohabitation cannot?

3. Given its obvious uniqueness, how does the symbol of the ultimate marriage make you want to respond?

6

UNEXPECTED
BENEFITS

We've covered the point of marriage and a few of the many reasons for it. I'd like to finish this section with some practical (while somewhat unexpected) benefits of marriage, now that all my cards are on the table so to speak.

A consistent and undeniable mountain of research, stretching all the way back to the 1970s and beyond, claims that marriage boosts every measure of human welfare. One journalist writes, "Marriage strongly boosts every important measure of well-being for children, women, and men. Pick any measure you can imagine: overall physical and mental health, income, savings, employment, educational success, general life contentment and happiness, sexual satisfaction, even recovery from serious disease, healthy diet and exercise. Married people rate markedly and consistently better in each of these, and so many more, compared to their single, divorced, and cohabiting peers. Thus, marriage is an essential active ingredient in improving one's overall life prospects, regardless of class, race, or educational status."[27]

Wow. That's quite the five-star review for marriage. Now, the research itself doesn't promise you a life free

MARRIAGE BOOSTS EVERY MEASURE OF HUMAN WELFARE.

from problems when/if you get married, of course. Hardships, trials, and suffering are always going to be a part of the human experience regardless of relationship status. However, the odds are certainly in your favor when it comes to well-being if you're wearing a wedding ring. Let's talk about a few of the reasons why.

COMMITMENT

Commitment? Ahh! Run away!

Commitment is a word that some avoid using because of the baggage that can often be associated with it. Phrases like "tied down," "trapped," or "held back" are often linked to commitment, and that simply doesn't mesh with western individualism. But commitment, when observed through a healthy connection to another person in marriage, is not just a good thing but a great thing.

Take sex for example. Sex within marriage is life-giving. It is the gracious, God-created plan for the maximum experience two people can have because they know that they aren't going anywhere. They know that within their marriage, there isn't any embarrassment or comparison or insecurity. They know that the other person isn't going to grab their clothes and leave in the morning. There is no walk of shame for married couples because they've committed their lives to each other in every way, not just sexually.[28] Commitment, in this case, ushers in health, acceptance, and security—the very opposite of being trapped or held back.

This is only one way of looking at commitment that turns the negative connotation on its head. In fact, I'd argue that the troubles that can regularly come with things such as money, raising children, physical health, isolation, extended family, anxiety, and addiction are diminished because of marriage commitment. Contrary to the negative knee-jerk reaction when one hears the word "commitment," in reality, it can be a phenomenal thing.

> COMMITMENT, IN THIS CASE, USHERS IN HEALTH, ACCEPTANCE, AND SECURITY— THE VERY OPPOSITE OF BEING TRAPPED OR HELD BACK.

MENTAL HEALTH

Mental health has become a public topic. Whereas it was once taboo to discuss such subjects anywhere outside of a therapist's office or the privacy of your own home, I've found that college students are now extremely comfortable talking over their mental health struggles with other people.

And, rightly so. I started having regular talks with an older trusted friend of mine a few years back, and my conversations with him have been tremendously helpful for processing my emotions, decreasing my stress, and working through my issues in a wholesome way. My appointments with him are often the times in my schedule that I look forward to the most because of how rich and deep they are.

And that kind of depth is also present in my marriage. I've found that being open with my wife about the internal struggles that plague me is one of the best things to protect my mental health. When we are forthright with each other about our struggles within, it's extremely therapeutic for both of us. And we're not alone. One publication says, "Marriage is good for your mental health. Married men and women are less depressed, less anxious, and less psychologically distressed than single, divorced, or widowed Americans."[29]

Additionally, once the factor of kids gets thrown into the mix, marriage—over simply living together—wins when it comes to the stresses of motherhood that can easily contribute to mental health problems. In fact, "Research shows that women are less stressed about their parental responsibilities if they live with their child's biological father, according to [Princeton University's] The Future of Children report. Conversely, single parenthood or relationships with new men increase their stress. And even if an unmarried woman lives with her child's father, it is likely they will not stay together—meaning that she will eventually face more stress, the report said."[30]

Marriage improves the lives of spouses and bolsters the mental health of husbands and wives in a way that no other cohabiting relationship can.

PHYSICAL HEALTH

When I think about marriage, I don't often mentally jump right to being healthy physically, but it's true; marriage can save your life. According to the research, married people live longer and healthier lives.

When University of Chicago scholar Linda Waite and a colleague analyzed mortality distinctions in a large, nationally representative sample, they found what they call a sizeable "marriage gap" in longevity. The study showed that nine out of ten married guys who are alive at age 48 will make it to the age of retirement at 65, compared with just six in ten comparable single guys (controlling for race, education, and income). For women, the benefits of marriage are also quite poignant, though not as large as they are for men. They found that nine out of ten wives alive at age 48 will live to be 65, compared with just eight out of ten cohabiting, single, or divorced women.[31]

> MARRIAGE IMPROVES THE LIVES OF SPOUSES AND BOLSTERS THE MENTAL HEALTH OF HUSBANDS AND WIVES IN A WAY THAT NO OTHER COHABITING RELATIONSHIP CAN.

It doesn't really get the press, but apparently marriage along with cardio and eating your green vegetables is good for your health.

STABILITY

As I mentioned before, my parents divorced when I was four years old, and from the time I started kindergarten all the way up to my early teens, my younger sister and I split time with each of our parents. We lived with our mom during the school year and every summer had a two-month visitation with our father.

Some years later, my mom married my stepdad (whom I call my dad); he was in the Air Force. So, because of the summer visitation each year, my sister and I found ourselves flying sometimes from halfway around the world by ourselves to see our father. I grew up highly anxious about almost everything because of the lack of stability in our family.

Don't get me wrong, it wasn't all bad (I got to live on the island of Guam for two years). But the lack of balance from an early age certainly contributed to many negative consequences in my life and has been deeply impactful when it comes to childhood wounds.

A friend of mine lives with her fiancé, and I've seen up close how her teenaged kids cope with the constant instability in their household. Many of the issues I see her kids wrestling with appear to be ten times worse than what my sister and I had to go through when we were children. Depression, anxiety, alcohol and marijuana abuse, panic attacks, and dropping out of school have all been a part of their experience.

Stability for a young person is a vital part of healthy development, and marriage provides that where cohabitation cannot. One writer notes, "Children benefit the most if their biological parents are married when they are born. . . . They are more likely to reap the benefits of their family's health insurance, higher income, and home ownership. When parents are more . . . stable, their children grow up with more resources, such as medical care and educational opportunities."[32]

PLENTIFUL BENEFITS

As the quote at the beginning of this chapter said, "Pick any measure you can imagine: overall physical and mental health, income, savings, employment, educational success, general life contentment and happiness, sexual satisfaction, even recovery from serious disease, healthy diet and exercise."[33]

The benefits of marriage are plentiful. The research proves it along with the personal stories of friends and family. Additionally, the Bible tells us that marriage inspires rejoicing (Isaiah 62:5), fosters an environment of love, giving, and mutual self-sacrifice (Ephesians 5:22-33), creates unrivaled companionship (Genesis 2:18), creates purposeful sexual intimacy (Proverbs 5:18-19), and establishes an environment of love and respect (1 Corinthians 13:4-8).

No doubt you have a number of examples surrounding you right now that you could observe and decide what makes more sense: living together or marriage. Hopefully, we have been able to examine it well enough here in order to persuade you of the merits of marriage.

UNEXPECTED BENEFITS-

1. Why do you think commitment is categorized as a benefit in this chapter as opposed to a burden?

2. In our angst-riddled world, how can marriage counteract anxiety's effects and provide stability for people who crave peacefulness and support?

3. How does the stability or instability of your child-hood influence the desire for your future children to live in an environment of balance and peace?

CONCLUSION

My hope and prayer is that you will be convicted of the truth that marriage is the all-around better route to take when it comes to your romantic relationship. Sure, moving in together is certainly the easy choice when it comes to noncommittal next steps with a significant other, but as the great fictional philosopher-wizard Albus Dumbledore once said, "Soon we must all choose between what is right and what is easy."[34]

Despite what the advertising world might tell you, easier is not always better. The things that take time, effort, and intentionality are often the things that move us more profoundly, and stick with us in our hearts. My relationship with God, for example, hasn't been an easy relationship—quite the opposite! I've been a Christian since my freshman year of college, and my life since making that decision has been characterized by many wrestling matches with Him. It has taken time, effort, and intentionality . . . and consequently has been the most profoundly moving relationship of my entire life. It has been *the* defining relationship that has spilled over into all my other relationships, including my most important earthly one with my wife.

And while being in relationship with God as a Christian has been hard, I've never once regretted giving my life to Him. My union with Christ has been the most fulfilling relationship to me, and I love it so much that I just have to talk about it.

Have you ever eaten a meal at a certain restaurant that just blew you away by how good it was? Did you love the meal so much that you just couldn't help talking about it to other people, demanding that they eat it too so they could share in the joy and pleasure of that food? Marriage is kind of like that meal for me—with both my wife and with Christ. Hopefully I've been able to describe "the meal" to you in such a way that you desire to partake of it too.

I encourage you not to settle for the inferior meal of cohabitation, but instead wonderfully dine on the joys of a committed relationship in marriage. Marriage isn't just a "piece of paper" telling the world that you love someone—that's the wedding certificate. Marriage is a life lived with another person that shows the watching world what it means to stick with someone despite the inevitable ups and downs that come with fluctuating circumstances and wavering emotions.

My relationship with God through Jesus has been what I've built my life upon, and that foundation has made it possible for me to focus on my marriage commitment to my wife when life is great and when my circumstances are simply awful. He's the reason it works.

WHAT'S THE NEXT POINT?

Still have questions about cohabitation or marriage? Wondering, *How does this apply to my relationship?*

You want to talk to your friends who are (or are considering) moving in together before marriage . . . *But how do I talk to them about it without them hating me?*

Or you have questions about God and faith.

You've got questions, we've got answers.

Find these and more at FamilyLife.com/NextPoint.

FOR FURTHER CONTENT

If you're curious about researching further into the subject of marriage and its merits or what it means to have a relationship with God, you'll likely want to know more.

 ## MARRIAGE

FamilyLife.com | They cover everything from date night ideas to porn addiction to fighting well to divorce to blended families, and so much more.

 ## KNOWING GOD

EveryStudent.com | There are articles and postings concerning the myriad of questions a skeptic can have when seeking answers about God.

EveryPerson.com | Visit to find an extensive amount of content on the subject of knowing God personally, and for a safe place online to ask questions/seek answers.

StartingWithGod.com | This site authentically helps guide you through the initial stages of getting to know God better.

NOTES

1. Benjamin Gurrentz, "Living with an Unmarried Partner Now Common for Young Adults," *United States Census Bureau*, November 15, 2018, https://www.census.gov/library/stories/2018/11/cohabitaiton-is-up-marriage-is-down-for-young-adults.html.

2. Mariah Sanders, Julie H. Haupt, Jeffrey Dew, Timothy Smith, "Cohabitation: Safety Net or Stability Threat?," *Institute for Family Studies*, February 3, 2020, https//ifstudies.org/blog/cohabitation-safety-net-or-stability-threat.

3. Sanders, Haupt, Dew, Smith, "Cohabitation."

4. Michael J. Rosenfeld, Katharina Roesler, "Cohabitation Experience and Cohabitation's Association With Marital Dissolution," *NCFR Journal of Marriage and Family*, September 24, 2018, accessed through Wiley Online Library at https://onlinelibrary.wiley.com/doi/full/10.1111/jomf.12530.

5. Scott M. Stanley, Galena Kline Rhoades, Howard J. Markman, "Sliding Versus Deciding: Inertia and the Premarital Cohabitation Effect," *NCFR Family Relations Interdisciplinary Journal of Applied Family Science*, September 7, 2006, accessed through Wiley Online Library at https://onlinelibrary.wiley.com/doi/full/10.1111/j.1741-3729.2006.00418.x.

6. Meg Jay, "The Downside of Cohabiting Before

Marriage," *The New York Times*, April 14, 2012, https://www.nytimes.com/2012/04/15/opinion/sunday/the-downside-of-cohabiting-before-marriage.html.

7. Jay, "The Downside."

8. Jay, "The Downside."

9. Sanders, Haupt, Dew, Smith, "Cohabitation."

10. Sanders, Haupt, Dew, Smith, "Cohabitation."

11. Glenn T. Stanton, "The Research Proves The No. 1 Social Justice Imperative Is Marriage," *The Federalist*, November 3, 2017, https://thefederalist.com/2017/11/03/research-proves-no-1-social-justice-imperative-marriage/.

12. Stanton, "The Research Proves."

13. "The State of Our Unions: Marriage in America 2011," National Marriage Project at the University of Virginia and the Center for Marriage and Families at the Institute for American Values, http://national-marriageproject.org/wp-content/uploads/2012/05/Union_2011.pdf.

14. Stanton, "The Research Proves."

15. Jay, "The Downside."

16. Jay, "The Downside."

17. Jay, "The Downside."

18. 1 Corinthians 13:11 (English Standard Version).

19. Shelby Abbott, *DoubtLess: Because Faith is Hard* (Greensboro, NC: New Growth Press, 2020), 87.

20. Maggie Gallagher, "Why Marriage Is Good For You," *City Journal*, Autumn 2000, https://www.city-journal.org/html/why-marriage-good-you-12002.html.

21. Gallagher, "Why Marriage Is Good."

22. Shelby Abbott, *I Am a Tool (To Help With Your Dating Life)* (Orlando: Cru Press, 2014), 31-32.

23. Gallagher, "Why Marriage Is Good."

24. Casey Leins, "9 Reasons Why You Should Get Married, For Yourself and For America," *U.S. News & World Report*, December 18, 2019, https://www.usnews.com/news/slideshows/9-reasons-why-you-should-get-married-for-yourself-and-for-america?slide=8.

25. Kevin DeYoung, "Why Is 'Be True to Yourself' a Bad Philosophy?," *The Gospel Coalition*, December 17, 2019, https://www.thegospelcoalition.org/video/true-bad-philosophy/.

26. Joel Ryan, "The Church Is the Bride of Christ — What Does that Mean?," *Christianity.com*, August 16, 2019, https://www.christianity.com/wiki/church/the-church-is-the-bride-of-christ.html.

27. Stanton, "The Research Proves."

28. Shelby Abbott, *I Am a Tool (To Help With Your Dating*

Life) (Orlando: Cru Press, 2014), 30.

29. Gallagher, "Why Marriage Is Good."

30. Casey Leins, "9 Reasons."

31. Gallagher, "Why Marriage Is Good."

32. Casey Leins, "9 Reasons."

33. Stanton, "The Research Proves."

34. J.K. Rowling, *Harry Potter and the Goblet of Fire* (New York: Scholastic Press, 2000), 628.

FAMILY IS **AMAZING**

At FamilyLife, we believe a strong family changes its corner of the world. It alters you, your kids, and your kids' kids—even your community.

We exist to fortify one-of-a-kind families and marriages like yours. For over 40 years, we've been committed to filling your tank with God's Word to equip you to strengthen your most important relationships with God, spouse, and kids. So our events, resources, and radio programs aim to equip, energize, and tune your life.

We realize your family and the challenges you grapple with every day are as unique as a fingerprint. But your individual home matters immensely.

Lean on us, laugh with us, learn with us, grow closer to God with us at FamilyLife.com.

f @FamilyLifeMinistry   @FamilyLifeInsta   @FamilyLifeToday